COUNTRY LIVING

decorating with
baskets

ACCENTS FOR EVERY ROOM

COUNTRY LIVING

decorating with baskets

ACCENTS FOR EVERY ROOM

by **MARY CALDWELL**

principal photography by **JEFF MCNAMARA**

styling by **INGRID LEESS**

foreword by **NANCY MERNIT SORIANO**

HEARST BOOKS
A DIVISION OF STERLING PUBLISHING CO., INC.
NEW YORK

For *Country Living*
Editor-in-Chief, Nancy Mernit Soriano
Deputy Editor, Lawrence A. Bilotti
Design Director, Susan M. Netzel

Produced by Smallwood and Stewart, Inc., New York City
Art Director: Debra Sfetsios

The Library of Congress has catalogued the hardcover edition as follows:
Country living decorating with baskets / by the editors of Country Living.
        p. cm.
Includes index.
ISBN 0-688-17503-1
1. Baskets. 2. Interior decoration. I. Country living (New York, N.Y.)
NK3649.5.C68 2000
747'.9—dc21   00-020495

First Paperback Edition 2005

10 9 8 7 6 5 4 3 2 1

Published by Hearst Books
A Division of Sterling Publishing Co., Inc.
387 Park Avenue South, New York, NY 10016

Photographs on pages 9, 13, 24, 26, 32, 38, 39, 40, 43, 52, 64, 67, 73, 80, 82, 83, 97, 100, 102, 103, 104, 106 by Keith Scott Morton: 20, 30, 33, 62-63 by Jessie Walker; 10-12, 37, 65, 91 by Stephen Randazzo; 34 by Pizzi/Thompson Associates; 47 by Gridley & Graves; 68 by William P. Steele; 78, 79 by John Blais; 90 by Julie Maris/Semel; 66 by Debra De Boise; all photographs styled by the editors of *Country Living*.

Cover photographs by Jeff McNamara

www.countryliving.com

Distributed in Canada by Sterling Publishing
c/o Canadian Manda Group, 165 Dufferin Street
Toronto, Ontario, Canada M6K 3H6

Distributed in Australia by Capricorn Link (Australia) Pty. Ltd.
P.O. Box 704, Windsor, NSW 2756 Australia

Printed in China

ISBN 1-58816-438-1

TABLE OF contents

foreword

WHEN I THINK ABOUT THE BASKETS I HAVE IN MY HOME and the ones that surround me in my office, I am amazed at the versatility of these woven objects. In addition to providing purely decorative accents, they continue to serve the purpose for which they were intended, namely, practical storage. From kitchen to bath, from bedroom to home office, baskets—whether old or new, and regardless of their original intent—are the perfect complement to any home, any room of the house.

In addition to being decorative and practical, baskets also connect us to our past, to a simpler time when handmade objects were the order of the day. Although many early baskets have become rare and highly collectible, we continue to find young artisans around the country who are making new examples true to traditional techniques.

Here at *Country Living*, our admiration for baskets—and for the artisans who make them—has been steadfast. For this book, we have collected some of the most beautiful and inventive examples we've encountered, both in our professional and personal lives. We share them with the hope that they'll inspire you to indulge in the pleasures of baskets in your home.

—NANCY MERNIT SORIANO

Editor-in-Chief

display

DID OUR ANCESTORS OBSERVE birds in the wild and learn to weave baskets by mimicking the way they built their nests? How baskets have evolved since the first crude vessels woven thousands of years ago! Some may still resemble birds' nests—creations lovely in themselves—but so many others exhibit remarkably refined shapes and patterns. And while baskets continue to offer utilitarian solutions for household needs, they are most often used around the home for the sheer pleasure of their handcrafted beauty.

Some basket collectors concentrate on a single style or period, perhaps Pennsylvania baskets from the mid-1800s, authentic Adirondack packs, nesting Nantucket lightship baskets, coiled Native American vessels, or avant-garde one-of-a-kind works of art made by contemporary artisans. If you are interested in either Shaker, Nantucket, or

Baskets are versatile decorations, shifting smoothly from season to season. The rich tones of an Indonesian twill-weave trunk (opposite) harmonize with a crisp summer slipcover and warm paisley throw. The trunk doubles as an end table while a nineteenth-century basket adds a step that continues the woven look. Wire mesh baskets too have a year-round appeal (above), whether filled with a jug of roses or grouping of pillar candles.

On a stairwell (opposite), a collection of urn-shaped Venezuelan coiled baskets lend fluid curves, rich pattern, and subtle texture to the vertical architecture. Intricately patterned Venezuelan baskets made by the Makitare Indians have an hourglass shape that is reminiscent of vessels thrown on a potter's wheel (above). A single shelf installed over a doorway turns a blank spot into a gallery for these pieces. A large and unusually detailed round winnowing basket nestles between them.

southwestern Native American baskets, you are in good company; these are considered to be among the most highly collectible baskets on the market today.

Many homeowners, however, have an eclectic collection of shapes and sizes that has been accumulated, rather than purposefully collected, over time. Whether you have a deliberate collection or a wonderful assortment, how you display your baskets depends on the style or mood desired.

A big basket conveys a bold statement and makes a dramatic impact. Experiment with placement: Do you get a stronger impression from a grouping of several large baskets, or when you display each one as a soloist, to emphasize its individual lines? Look for unexpected spots to showcase the collection. A tall basket can make a dim corner spring to life or transform an empty landing into a splendid gallery.

For a homey, rural feeling, choose country style baskets that have some rusticity, like natural finishes or evidence of farmhouse and agricultural use. Group them informally on a table or in an open cupboard, or hang them from hooks mounted on the ceiling.

THE ARTIST AS BASKET MAKER

For many contemporary basket makers, the ancient craft of making functional objects has evolved into pure art. Rather than having a particular use in mind and following a traditional pattern, artist Nina Payne began instead with the materials as her inspiration.

For Payne, a poet and college professor who resides in Amherst, Massachusetts, basket making began when a sculptor friend introduced her to waxed linen from an electrical supply house around the same time her mother-in-law taught her to crochet. Like most weavers, her first designs were regular, symmetrical containers, and she then added lids. "I just loved working with the waxed linen because it seemed to yield something new each time I approached it. It was the right material for me."

Later Payne discovered even more ways to push the boundaries with her crochet hook. Coming across a basket she made that had accidentally collapsed of its own weight, she found beauty and intrigue in the new shape, and thus altered her approach. "It evolved as I went along," she says. The process of discovery is based partly on the material and the particular configuration that it produced—but, mostly, on the imagination of the artist.

Lacquered baskets from Asia—where the lacquer tree grows indigenously—can set a tailored or formal mood and lend an international flavor to a decor. Similarly, the finish on a basket of authentic African heritage is often made from fruit pulp, a material which is readily available in some areas of the continent. Woven or coiled baskets of African, South American, or Native American origin, especially those in distinctive colors or embellished with indigenous motifs, introduce interesting cultural notes.

BASKET REGALIA

It's both easy and fun to decorate favorite baskets around the home, dressing them up to match your mood, the season, a holiday, or the theme of a party. Fill a large basket with multi-colored tissue paper or shredded wrapping-paper confetti—this makes a festive nest for Champagne glasses at an intimate cocktail party.

Wrap ribbon, in a color to suit the occasion, around a basket's handle. Luxurious, exquisitely colored French ribbon (also called florist's ribbon), which has thin wire running through its length, bends easily and holds its shape well. If the weave of the basket is loose enough to allow it, thread a ribbon or crepe paper through the openings.

A *twined willow basket filled with a surplus of black-and-white throw pillows adds just the right touch at the end of a white couch. The mix-and-match patterning of the pillows adds interest to the room while the light-colored natural hue of the basket injects warmth and subtle color.*

BASKET SHOWCASE

Almost all baskets take naturally to the spotlight when you display them. Keep an open mind and don't always follow the practical intentions of the basket maker.

FEATURE trays as pictures, complete with their own frames. Hang them individually or try arranging several in different sizes and colors in a column on a narrow wall between doorways. Mount a large round tray between a pair of smaller round mirrors or sconces.

STORE brushes, pencils, tubes of paint, and other artist's tools in beaker-shaped baskets; always line the baskets beforehand with plastic to protect them from paint and other potentially harmful residues.

DISPLAY a collection of baskets along a fireplace mantel—alone or mixed with other objects like pillar candles, framed photographs, and art pottery. Stack pine cones or woven-rattan balls in flower-gathering baskets in an empty hearth.

With wire or ribbon, tie seasonal decorations on the handle or rim—jingle bells or candy canes for Christmas; paper hearts and red roses for Valentine's Day. Sprigs of handpicked shamrocks are pretty tied to a basket handle with raffia for St. Patrick's Day.

To serve bread, rolls, crackers, or small sandwiches at a party, line a basket with fabric. In the tradition of European bakeries that use linen-lined baskets to hold rising bread, simply smooth a linen napkin into a basket. For a tailored approach, sew in a lining—fold the fabric once over the rim and stitch it through the weave of the basket with sturdy thread.

The doors on a country-style corner cupboard are opened wide to show off the collection of splint-work baskets stowed within. The bottom-most basket is an oval-shaped version made by plaiting thin splints. The two on the shelves above and the one on top of the cupboard also are made of splints that are extra large and painted. The spokes are uniquely held in place on this color-rinsed trio with metal bands of varying widths.

21

N atural elements coordinate well with baskets. A French bread basket filled with thatch reeds brightens the hearth in a monochromatic arrangement that includes a farmer's roughly woven straw work basket and wine bottles covered with chestnut and rattan (above). Baskets of all shapes and sizes are strewn along shelves in combination with a variety of natural items—such as the collection of butterflies—for interest (opposite).

Stencil or hand paint a motif—the outline of an oak leaf, a small fleur de lis, or a twisting green vine—onto a wide wooden basket handle or a wood-splint basket. Or use a simple repeating pattern such as dots or fine stripes to decorate the whole basket.

To welcome spring, swirl strands of ivy or fresh flowers through an open-weave basket or around a handle. Use florist's tubes to ensure that the blooms stay fresh.

Hot-glue decorative objects and small mementos to the surface of the basket to create a theme: buttons and satin ribbons for a seamstress, twig pencils for a writer, miniature cookie cutters and whisks for a baker.

Dressing up a basket can also mean turning it into a vase. In ancient times, woven vessels worked just fine for toting berries or nuts, but gaps in the weave made it tricky to haul water or other liquids. So the inside of the basket was painted with a waterproofing agent.

The Old Testament's Book of Exodus, for example, tells the story of the infant Moses being concealed from Pharaoh in "a basket made of bulrushes . . . daubed with bitumen and pitch" to keep the baby safe and dry as he was hidden "among the reeds at the river's brink." Nowadays, an unassuming plastic or metal liner can easily waterproof a basket and turn it into a planter or a vase.

NATURAL PARTNERS

Baskets of natural materials have a special affinity for nature's offerings. Displays can range from tiny baskets holding a few polished stones or homemade lavendar potpourri to large wicker umbrella stands showing off tall branches of curly willow, stalks of autumn corn, or bundles of lanky marsh cattails. When creating pairings, think about the material, color, and texture of the basket and what would complement it. Look around in your yard or garden or in the woods for materials to be gathered.

If you happen to find a one-of-a-kind item like an abandoned bird's nest, show it off in a basket with sides that are shallow enough to permit viewing without having to handle it. Or fill a rustic basket roughly woven of small oak branches with feathers of various colors and shapes collected during nature walks.

Hang flat-backed Adirondack guide packs or vintage fishing creels from hooks or pegs to create a display of seasonal items in a foyer. In the spring, nestle pastel-colored eggs in a lush bed of fresh wheatgrass; in summer, choose ripe fruit and vegetables or a few medium-size sunflowers. In autumn, arrange pumpkin vines and leaves of various shapes and colors, and in the winter, try a mixture of pinecones and evergreeens.

H igh ceilings present the perfect opportunity to display delicate or damaged baskets in a prominent, yet out-of-reach, location. Experiment with the space and give special attention to the arrangement of the baskets within it. The openness above a set of French doors is maximized by varying placement of large baskets— horizontally, vertically, bottoms up—to heighten the visual interest and impact of the display.

A trug, designed to hold flowers as they are cut in the garden, is a wide, flat basket with slightly raised sides and a handle. One would look pretty on a side table with dried flowers, fresh herbs, evergreen boughs, or holly branches. Or play against type and use a small trug to cradle stones gathered from a stream bed. Contrasting different natural materials—hard and soft, symmetrical and imperfect—can prove equally as visually dynamic as complementing them.

In the winter, decorate a mantelpiece or a sideboard with a series of baskets that increase gradually in size, each filled with pinecones in similarly increasing sizes. Or gather other natural materials that are in season such as sweet-gum-tree spurs, miniature ears of Indian corn, or a pile of chestnuts.

Perhaps the material of the basket and the objects that fill it come from the same environment or even the same plant. A seagrass basket might hold all kinds of shells, strands of dried palm and kelp, bits of driftwood, and pebbles and sea glass ground smooth by the ocean's waves. What could tell a more complete story than an oak splint basket laden with leaves and acorns?

B askets are more than just utilitarian consolidators; they also unite decorative elements into a harmonious design. For a nature-inspired centerpiece on a seasonal table, pear-shaped candles surround a basket filled with grape hyacinths (above). Life imitates art: A trio of framed botanical prints makes a suitable backdrop for willow pedestal baskets piled with fruit (opposite). Pedestals also make wonderful dessert stands for a cake, a tart, or a stack of cookies.

CREATING A GALLERY

If your basket collection has grown quite large, maximize the visual impact by grouping the baskets for display. Choose your favorites—it doesn't matter if some are natural-colored and some painted or stained, some antique and some new. Even baskets that have sustained considerable wear or damage have a certain visual charm.

Improvise a display on a tiered plant stand, wooden step stool, or small stepladder. Open the stool and ladder or leave them closed, leaning them upright against a wall. Vary the look by grouping the baskets from tallest to smallest or by juxtaposing sizes randomly.

Hang handled baskets from a standard hat rack or coat tree. Or mount them on stands designed specially for displaying baskets; these stands have more arms than a regular coat tree and they are placed at varying levels.

The Shakers furnished the walls of their rooms with practical rows of pegs for hanging all manner of household goods, including the chairs when it was time to sweep the floor. Shaker pegs, or similar rows of hooks, easily and attractively hold favorite baskets.

Group baskets to liven up and give drama to empty or unlikely spots—along the wall in entry halls; on top of chests of drawers or bathroom vanities; in an untrafficked

Sold as a waste basket, a willow container makes an intriguing lantern when it is filled with pillar candles of varying sizes. The glow of candlelight filtering through the screen-like openwork weave casts variegated shadows, creating a centerpiece effect more exotic than tapers in candlesticks. When using candles and baskets together, be absolutely sure that there's plenty of clearance between the flame and the basket, which is highly flammable, and never leave candles unattended when lit.

corner of the living room; on a staircase, parading down one at a time; or along a seat in a picture window.

Imagine woven trays as framed pictures. Get them off tables and out of cupboards and hang them in groupings on walls. You can frame them or let each stand on its own as a unique and charming objet d'art. Try arranging three baskets in different sizes and colors in a column on a narrow wall between doorways, or hang a large round winnowing basket between a pair of smaller, similar-colored round mirrors or sconces.

Instead of ordinary-looking jars and crocks to store brushes, pencils, and other artist's tools, select an arrangement of beaker-shaped baskets. Arrange centerpieces of pillar candles in low, flat baskets or in taller, openwork baskets. Give an old-fashioned hurricane lantern an indoor makeover by nestling it inside a close-fitting basket. Consider any basket as a cachepot for a blooming plant or bouquet of flowers.

Traditional gift baskets full of fruit or cheeses or candies are always a delight to assemble and to receive, but for other gifts as well, try using a decorated basket instead of a box and wrapping paper: enfold a sweater in tissue paper, tie it once with twine, and present it in a rectangular hand basket—which becomes part of the gift.

T*he presence of picnic baskets on a table set for a relaxed afternoon gathering conjures the mood of a summer idyll. At a party, a basket can hold fresh flowers, conceal extra necessities such as napkins, glassware, candles, and cutlery, or reign as an object of beauty to delight the eye.*

*W*here a chest might otherwise
stand, varied baskets—most
made of oak— straddle an antique
clothes drying rack (opposite).
The melon basket holding balls of
fabric has a striking, God's Eye
design, classically placed where the
handle and the rim intersect.
Baskets placed sparingly on a rough,
country shelf made of thin trees
and branches are showcased—
standing out beautifully against
the dark bark of the shelving and the
room's pale yellow wall (above).

COLLECTIBLE CLASSICS

People collect baskets for many reasons. The direction of their collecting is usually an extension of their own interests—perhaps in contemporary crafts or rural life in the nineteenth century—that leads them to a particular style, such as Appalachian, Shaker, Nantucket, Native American, or a combination of weaves that reflect different world cultures or techniques.

Many contemporary collectors are enamored with the search for American splint baskets crafted of hardwoods by both Native Americans and the eighteenth-century European settlers. Oftentimes, the baskets of the settlers are folk arty pieces which were originally painted to enhance and brighten both a living space as well as the very days spent performing the daily farming chores.

Among the most important collectible baskets are those made by the Shakers, a religious sect that flourished in the 1800s and pioneered many styles of furniture and baskets that are quite popular today—woven-tape chair seats, wooden peg rails, swallowtail boxes, plain-fronted chests and cabinets. Shaker style—even that of so-called Shaker fancy baskets—is characterized by its practicality and clean, simple lines lacking in fussy details.

L ight and contrast are truly essential to any display of objects or art. By suspending a row of splint baskets along the tops of a room's windows, the homeowner allows sun to highlight the patterns of the weaves while simultaneously creating an unusual valance. The drama is increased by the S-hooks attaching the baskets, which are crafted of graceful wrought iron, their curves a clever contrast the the linear basket weaves.

IN THE KITCHEN

Natural baskets made for specific kitchen duties abound, and often provide an attractive alternative to plastic and other synthetics. A woven cutlery tray, for example, looks good in a kitchen drawer and on a buffet or patio table. Other baskets can hold bottles of wine or, fitted with a waterproof liner, chill Champagne or function as an ice bucket. Divided baskets keep drinking glasses or several wine bottles from rattling into each other; they can also organize condiments and utensils to be ferried out to the backyard or patio. Carrying food—berries gathered in the woods or vegetables picked from the garden—ranks high among traditional basket duties.

Of course, any basket that you have can be pressed into service to organize napkins, meat tenderizers and grilling tools, cookbooks or recipe cards, or telephone message slips. Consider those functional handbaskets—usually made of thin splints of wood, such as poplar—that you might carry home from the local roadside farmstand, filled with ripe tomatoes or crisp, fall apples. Recycle them as countertop caddies for oils, vinegars, and all those other bottles that accumulate in the cooking area.

Fill a large basket with freshly-laundered kitchen towels, another with aprons, and tuck a third under a work

A line of willow baskets is hung on a narrow wall (opposite) to bring texture to an otherwise empty space. The purely decorative teapot on the table is a whimsical interpretation of a classic chicken-wire egg-collecting basket. A more traditional egg-collecting basket (above) wears its age into a graceful retirement.

well-stocked kitchen should always contain fresh garlic for creating zesty, flavorful dishes. A basket with a swing handle holds bulbs and cloves at the ready on a kitchen counter (above). A large winnowing basket is a spherical frame for a rope of garlic (opposite) hung next to an antique cupboard. The cupboard is decorated with another round basket also placed vertically to echo the theme, as well as a third basket, which functions as a drinks stand.

table or in a corner to catch the linens when they are ready for washing.

Baskets hung from the kitchen wall create instant and attractive displays. There is no limit to their uses, whether they are baskets made specifically for hanging or others adapted with flat backs to suit your needs. Keep rolled dish-towels near the sink in a wall basket—off wet counters and more accessible than in a drawer. Use wall baskets also to store unrefrigerated produce, like onions, garlic, and tomatoes.

Often overlooked in the basket department, the refrigerator can become much more organized with little work. Miniature baskets can give a refreshing facelift to ordinary tubs of butter and cream cheese that are transported to and from the table. Larger baskets offer an accessible way to collect and carry frequently used condiments out to the grill or to group produce items for quick and convenient salad-making.

When the inevitable spill occurs on a kitchen basket, prevent staining by cleaning it immediately with a mild dish detergent or other gentle soap. A vegetable scrubber works well on the delicate materials of a basket. Then, let the basket air dry thoroughly before returning it to duty.

O n an otherwise underutilized floorspace in a bright and spacious kitchen, a warm seasonal showcase is created by a doorway to the outdoors. An extra large basket holds branches of bittersweet that have been gathered in the backyard. With pumpkins of various sizes and extra branches arranged casually around the basket, the kitchen is dressed up enough to be viewed by visitors who spill over into the room at a relaxed afternoon party.

B askets naturally complement the clean look of a crisp white bedroom. A Philippine vase (above) anchors a froth of white hydrangeas. Double-handled picnic baskets painted white (opposite) are as collectible as they are pretty; the baskets look wonderful stacked as a tower on a windowsill in a delicately rustic bedroom.

IN THE BEDROOM

By definition a restful retreat, a bedroom is a place where baskets can contribute to a beautiful, peaceful setting. All kinds of wickerwork and other woven furniture have been designed to coordinate in the bedroom—chests of drawers, armoires, mirror frames, love seats, rockers, and other assorted chairs. To complete a look, simply place a basket on top of any piece of furniture that offers an empty space.

Baskets work well in literally any country bedroom decorating scheme. They warm up a cool white room, bring texture to play in panelled rooms, and add contrast to pastel floral bedlinens. Use an empty picture windowsill to highlight a special basket with strong details such as a handled openwork basket with unusually wide splints. Paint the basket in a shade that matches the colors of the bedroom. A pale blue basket complements deep blue paint; or use a bright sunshine yellow as a bold contrast.

You may be happy to know that there are plenty more ways to incorporate the beauty of decorative basketry. Folding wicker screens are readily available for use as a bedroom divider or as a backdrop centered behind a bed or a pretty pitcher on a nightstand. Window shades or lampshades woven of grasses, rattan, and reeds, in rustic or tailored styles lend an air of tropical or Eastern whimsy

to a bedroom. Tablecloths, curtains, and other soft furnishings with basket print or weave can also be adapted to enhance your decor. For instance, pair baskets with plaid, a classic interpretation of the woven look.

In a nursery, an antique woven cradle is the perfect opener for other woven textures. Lidded baskets under the cradle fill a space that otherwise can look dark and barren. Square or round flat baskets mounted on the walls are pretty frames for baby ephemera and those quickly outgrown caps and booties.

In a child's bedroom, basket decorating possibilities abound. For preschoolers, eliminate the look of messy clutter by embellishing a few sturdy baskets with a hand-painted or stenciled tag to identify the contents; even easier, cut out a picture of shoes or dolls to encourage children to fill the basket, for example, mount it between two sheets of clear self-sticking paper, and attach with a loop of colored yarn.

Teenagers express their first "decorating statements" in their bedrooms. Baskets are probably the most versatile device, appealing to people of all ages and infinitely changeable in appearance and application. Baskets from childhood can be repainted and hung from the ceiling, window frame, or wall. Stenciling and other decorative

I n a simply decorated room, a nightstand made of stacked baskets modeled after old fashioned willow luggage or picnic hampers introduces subtle texture without overwhelming the mood of calm. The natural warm tones of the basketry are a foil for the pristine white walls. A transferware serving platter serves as the table top, steadying both lamp and pitcher.

45

An eight-point star variation quilt is a luxurious focus for the center of a sunny, converted attic bedroom. However, it is in part the pattern of the weaves that gives the room its texture and deep warmth. A large twined basket with a long wooden base nicely rounds out an otherwise drab space creating visual interest and height with its presence above a rough country cupboard. A smaller plaited-splint basket below the nightstand harmonizes—filling a low space while simultaneously echoing the woven look.

techniques make personalizing baskets a creative pleasure. Tokens of affection and mementos of happy activities— shopping tags, airline boarding passes, theatre ticket stubs —can be gathered and glued to a basket to make it a unique scrapbook of a vacation. Flat baskets are particularly receptive to displaying photographs, post cards, and other paper memorabilia that, assembled together, becomes an artwork of memories.

In a guest bedroom, baskets are an inexpensive way to quickly add warmth and cohesion to the decor. Mount them on walls and shelves to give the room a fresh, welcoming glow. Load a small basket with miniature containers of soap, shampoo, lotion, powder, a sewing kit, and other overnight necessities, perhaps accompanied by a new pair of bath gloves or some other little luxury.

Stack several large square or rectangular baskets one on top of the other in a corner or other small space. Next to the bed, the stacked baskets become a unique nightstand. On the nightstand, arrange several current magazines or books of local interest tucked into another basket, and topped with a burst of flowers in a vase. Depending on the time of day that guests will be arriving, a goodnight snack or an assortment of goodies for afternoon tea is an inviting treat to behold.

*E*ven a humble mending kit *seems worthy of display and notice if nestled in a picturesque coiled lidded basket. The homey tabletop tableau includes a rattan basket bursting with Queen Anne's lace, which was arranged in a watertight container set into the basket. Combined to complement other objects of similar tones, such as an old wood spool now acting as a candlestick, a framed picture, and a stack of painted boxes, baskets show off their textural and sculptural qualities even while performing their everyday function.*

IN THE BATHROOM

Perhaps more than any other room in the house, bathrooms can benefit from the warm, softening qualities of baskets. Conveniently, the bathroom is actually a supportive environment for most baskets, because the humidity from the shower or the bathtub prevents the reed, wood, and other materials from completely drying out. And too, there are dozens of items that need to be kept close at hand but do not merit prominent display.

Though wickerwork accessories have been designed just for the bathroom, including shelving, cabinets, and facial tissue holders, you can also choose your favorite large or small woven containers to provide graphic interest, or to hold laundry, toiletries, boxes of extra facial tissue, and cleaning supplies. Wickerwork pieces can also supplement the linen closet.

Fill many small baskets on the vanity with practical items such as bath salts, washcloths, combs, hairbrushes, and soaps, or display a purely decorative collection of buttons, beads, or antique hair ornaments in them.

Larger baskets can fit directly under the sink or counter and right on the floor. Look for baskets that complement other shapes, textures, or colors in the room, such as a basket painted in a hue that matches a shower curtain.

A deep rectangular basket keeps a generous supply of towels handy at tubside; a smaller basket holds rolled-up washcloths. As echoes of the baskets, the woven-grass slippers are Indonesian, and the glass candle container has been wrapped with twine. Baskets like these in the bathroom are easy to carry about from tub to shower, from bath to laundry room.

51

In the shower or tub, coordinated plastic baskets organize soaps and cleaners, shampoos and conditioners, bath toys, scrub brushes, pumice stones, and shaving equipment. Baskets, happily, will not shatter as glass can, and in the bathroom especially this added safety feature is important.

A woven wall basket or wall pocket is a discreet holder for potpourri, sachets, or cotton balls spritzed with a favorite cologne. For more organic scents, fill the basket with freshly cut plants or flowers in a small jar of water.

In a bathroom that's short on space, collapsible wire hanging baskets designed for the kitchen can be quite handy. Often used to hold onions, garlic, and fruit, these multi-tiered baskets work well as hanging nests for larger soaps, washcloths, and toiletries. Share and share alike or designate each tier for a family member to sort his or her own necessities. Guests, too, will appreciate a spot of their own for toothbrushes and floss, brushes and combs, and their personal toiletries. Larger wire baskets, whether antique or the type found at office supply stores, are convenient for seasonal toiletries such as sunscreen and winter moisturizer, and a supply of toilet rolls. These baskets are available in many different sizes, making it possible to find one that will fit in the awkward space alongside so many toilets or on the shelves of a linen closet.

*T**he inspired placement of a single basket can bring balance to a spare, understated space. Under one of a pair of bamboo stools sits a bowl-shaped basket of rocks (above). Wall baskets for flowers, woven with a flat back, feature waterproof liners and hooks or loops. In summer, hang one on the wall and fill it daily with a garden bouquet (opposite).*

W ire baskets have the dual
advantages of sturdiness
and transparency, making them
perfect caddies for items you like
to see. A wire basket makes an
unexpected curio case, displaying
seashells and other objects that
capture the changing seasons—
gourds in autumn, rose hips in
winter, pussy willows for spring.

THE GREAT OUTDOORS

Perhaps the most natural home use for baskets is out-doors, where the affinity between life and function is strongest. On porches and patios, handcrafted baskets symbolize welcome. Further out in the yard, in the flower garden or near the pool, they are becoming counterparts to growing plants and glittering water. All but the most fragile baskets can remain outdoors, so long as they are elevated from soggy ground and not allowed to sit in pud-dles. To get the longest wear out of baskets for outdoor use, make sure they have a protective coating—paint or varnish—and avoid subjecting them to extreme fluctua-tions of temperature or humidity.

A sheltered porch is a good choice—during most of the year, the humidity outdoors will help prevent the bas-ket from drying out. Organize gardening tools, twine, and an assortment of seeds on the wall of a semi-enclosed porch. Hang flat-backed Adirondack guide packs from hooks or pegs to hold seasonal items by the porch door—in summertime, beach towels and beach blankets; in win-tertime, ski hats, mittens, scarves, and gloves.

In late winter or earliest spring, get a head start by forcing forsythia or flowering quince branches to bloom indoors. Then, weeks before the buds have opened on the

*O*n a covered porch, a delicate, free-form basket made of vines provides a nest for a cluster of small rosemary plants in terra-cotta pots. The graceful, whimsical vine basket contrasts handsomely with a pair of more formal urn-shaped willow baskets. Employing baskets in the same way—in this case holding herbal plants—is made complex and interesting when the basket weaves are so aesthetically different. Their proximity brings out their uniquely individual textures, emphasizing the richness of design that each offers.

shrubs in the yard, show off the glorious blossoms in baskets set outside the front door or along a walkway. In the summer, arrange geraniums and other potted plants nestled into baskets on a porch railing or stairway.

During temperate summer months, baskets full of cut flowers, potted annuals, or houseplants normally confined indoors for most of the year add a welcoming, homey touch to unexpected spots outside the house. Cascades of petunias and splashes of fuchsia look pretty hanging from soffit-mounted hooks or brackets fastened to the siding of the house or the porch ceiling.

Container gardens have long been a favorite of landscape designers, who utilize them to bring fresh plantings in as others fade, and to establish separate areas for entertaining, recreation, or storage. For a movable outdoor decoration, fill a wheelbarrow or a child's wagon with baskets of flowers and roll it to a spot in the yard that could use some brightening: beside the front steps, next to the picnic table, along a walkway, next to the gardening shed door.

For working in the garden, no tote looks better than a utilitarian basket, sturdy and fitted with a comfortable handle, to keep secateurs, trowel, gloves, plant tags, extra soil, and other essentials near at hand. As a bonus, the filled basket can be stored when work is done.

I nexpensive flat-reed baskets painted in a wash of white are great for collecting vegetables, herbs, and flowers in the garden. But they needn't be limited to gardening tasks: fit deep-sided ones with one or several watertight containers full of summer bouquets to set on a porch or kitchen table. Lush, exuberant hibiscus blooms make a nice contrast to the regular, rectilinear weave of the basket, creating a cool white-on-white display.

BASKETS IN WINTER

The bare branches of a winter tree evoke the beauty of twigs and stems that could be woven into next year's baskets. The sprays of bittersweet, gnarled grapevines, and curly willow of the cold weather landscape suggest wonderful creations for the weaver.

Baskets outdoors in winter are different: they are hardier, stronger, even a bit wizened. Firebaskets, whether they are woven ones for kindling or wrought-iron cradles for cut logs, impart the promise of warmth. On a much smaller scale, a letter basket, with a flutter of snow revealing holiday cards within, offers immense comfort. An old bushel basket heaped with walnuts softens the porch bench. Great big, deep baskets filled with a small forest of cut greens—pine boughs, juniper, holly, sumac, and winterberry—welcome guests. Fitted with miniature white lights, they are a sparkling beacon on winter's dreariest days and darkest nights. A pair of such baskets on either side of the front door issues a splendid invitation.

Whatever inspiration strikes you, remember that there is no wrong place for a basket: whether sited with intense deliberation or floated into place with pure whimsy, every basket is a joy to behold.

T*he most natural-looking containers for flowers and plants are baskets. Nestled in the crook of the tree, a petite antique berry basket cradling hot pink cosmos turns a backyard gathering into a cheerful garden-party. A modern lantern with a bright-pink candle has an unexpected presence hung against the rough bark of a fine old tree.*

function

service
AND
utility

FOR COUNTLESS GENERATIONS, baskets and basket making have served as a simple and elegant reflection of our humanity. Hand-crafted baskets of natural materials have never gone out of favor. As much about function as baskets are about art, they continue to contribute grace and beauty—not to mention practicality—to every room of the home. Diminutive or grand, rustic or refined, every basket has the charm of timeless appeal.

We may no longer require the practical service of baskets in the same ways that we used to—plastics, metals, ceramics, and even cardboard can all easily fulfill the basket's original role as a container for storing and toting. But of all these materials, natural baskets achieve perfection.

Ancient basket makers, who could only forage close to home for reeds, branches, vines, and grasses to weave or to

A generous fishing creel hangs on a mounted hook in an entry hall (opposite), while other fishing supplies rest nearby, ready for an impromptu daytrip to a wooded stream. A round, shallow basket placed in an entry is an easy way to keep the whole family organized (above). Gather up gloves at the beginning of a cold winter's day, and lie them back in the basket at the end of the outing.

B askets are always convenient receptacles for the daily mail that flows in and out of the home. A handled basket placed as a doorstop (opposite) doubles as a container for magazines and other mail. It can easily be carried to and from the office at sorting time. A painted wall basket with a flat back (above) is the perfect way to hold outgoing items. Mount one on the outside of a front door to receive the paper delivery each morning.

coil and stitch into utilitarian containers, would be astonished at the vast array of supplies, styles, and baskets that are available worldwide today. Contemporary basket makers are mixing and matching styles, weaves, materials, and colors in innovatively and dynamically modern ways. While some basket makers are happy to push the envelope of modernity, others pride themselves on being able to render traditional-style baskets with historical accuracy and precision.

Whatever its source, whatever its style, a basket speaks of creativity, skill, and our abiding connection with nature. In the home, even new baskets somehow harken back to earlier generations. Every group in America—Native Americans, Europeans, Asians, and Africans—has a strong tradition of basket making. Woven of ordinary twigs and weeds, often with untrained hands, a basket is a supreme example of the sum being greater than its parts.

BASKET MATERIALS

What are baskets made of? Almost any pliable material can be woven into a basket. Depending on the intended design and use of the basket, materials range from the strictly traditional willow branches, twigs, and split reeds to the

imaginatively artful sea grasses, grave vines, cotton and linen cording, and even feathers.

Many baskets are woven of rattan, a tropical palm vine that bears a resemblance to bamboo, except that it has a solid core. Rattan grows rapidly in Indonesia and other parts of Southeast Asia. It is inexpensive, flexible, and abundant. Thin rattan poles are chosen for weaving baskets and the rattan core can be split into numerous cuts of reed for basket weaving.

Baskets are also made from tree bark, leaves, curly willow, raffia, straw, corn husk, and waxed linen. Fiber rush made of paper twisted around wire was popular as an inexpensive alternative to willow wickerwork in the United States early in the 1900s.

Splints made of hardwoods such as ash, oak, and poplar are widely favored as weavers and sometimes as spokes. Sliced from a tree trunk into flat thin strips, splints are first soaked in water until the wood is sufficiently flexible for weaving.

The type of material in an antique basket can indicate where it was made. In classifying baskets of the United States, for example, splint work is linked to the northeast and central Atlantic regions where forests are prolific, while coilwork is linked to the grasslands.

Natural materials—such as fireplace logs and rattanwork harmoniously beside a living room hearth. The big tub-shaped basket helps keep the room neat by catching those little bits of bark and kindling that so often litter the floor around open log bins. And because the basket is comparatively lightweight, it can easily be turned over and shaken clean outdoors.

WOVEN ART

The art of weaving enhances far more than utilitarian containers. Woven textures are so beautiful in lampshades, cane seats, tote bags and sandals, even as a motif in fabric design.

WIDE-brimmed floppy straw hats with colorful ribbons bring a natural romance to a sewing room or bedroom. English splint bonnets from the early nineteenth century are highly prized, as are the English woven bonnets crafted by the Pennsylvania Quakers.

FLAT mats specifically designed as placemats have a squared-off shape to accommodate an array of silverware and plates. Fans made of palm-leaf add a decorative flair as mats in table settings; they can also be mounted on a wall, alone or in groupings.

WINE or seltzer bottles covered in basketry are a pretty way to add variety to a display of glass bottles. The bottle-in-basket idea first evolved as a way to protect bottles from breakage. Pitchers and thermoses in baskets are attractive additions to a bartop collection.

ANTIQUE cradles have a strong presence on their own but take on more beauty brimming with pretty linens, flowers, or porcelain dolls. Basketweave folding screens too have the ability to fit into any room and any season.

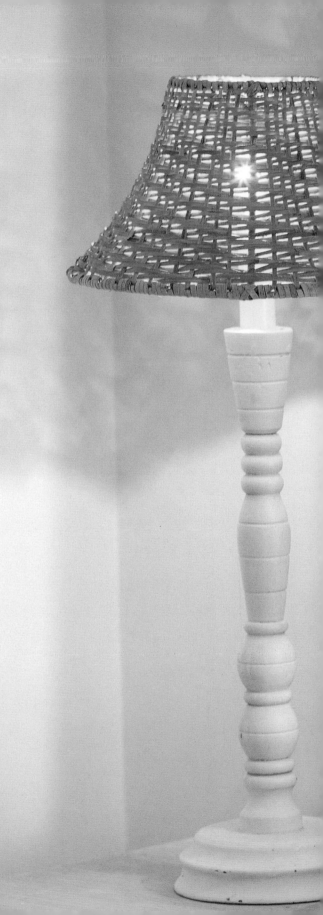

TEXTILE STORAGE TIPS

CHECK the basket thoroughly for rough reeds or a stray bit of wire that could snag or rip delicate fabrics before choosing it for textile storage. Run your fingers around the inside to isolate problem areas. With fine sanding paper, lightly smooth out any small burrs or nicks.

CHOOSE rattan baskets with a sheen or lacquered appearance. Rattan, without this protective coating, is highly susceptible to mold, which will damage fabrics.

STORE quilts, afghans, throw pillows, and other textiles in decorative baskets so they are handy, not hidden. Because they allow air to circulate freely, woven baskets for fabrics are vastly preferable to sealed plastic storage containers, which set stains and encourage mold, mildew, and discoloration.

ADAPT baskets as drawers in a linen closet and fill them with smaller items like tea cloths, table runners, and vintage luncheon napkins.

A *pair of rattan storage baskets from Indonesia keeps a collection of pretty quilts tucked away but, thanks to the openwork sides, on view and accessible to circulating air. Though the baskets may resemble antiques, they are contemporary and readily available from retailers. The diagonally plaited nesting baskets on the table can be pressed into countless uses.*

Pine needle baskets are made by arranging overlapping bundles of pine needles to form a long rope that's coiled and then stitched to hold its shape. This technique requires great care to keep the bundle of needles evenly sized as the coil grows and results in a basket that is surprisingly heavy and dense.

Usually, species of pine boughs that have extra-long needles are preferred for coiling, as they are easier to capture in the stitches. The pine needles themselves may be green or brown, depending on whether they've been dried in light or dark conditions, and basket weavers have the option to remove the cap that connects each little clump

or to keep it and highlight its nubbiness, providing greater texture and a more rustic look.

BASKET TYPES

A complete catalog of all known basket shapes and styles would be impossible to compile, given the endless variations possible in handcrafting a creation. Here is a listing of some common shapes that you might encounter when browsing for baskets.

Melon baskets are similar in shape to a round melon cut in half. With spokes that radiate out from the base of the handle, melon baskets bear a strong resemblance to the pattern made by stripes on a watermelon. They are commonly thought to be the descendants of old world British gathering baskets.

Twin-bottomed egg baskets are shaped like melon baskets, but they have a pronounced division into two round pouches or cheeks. The double pouches were meant to keep eggs or other goods from rolling around and breaking as they were gathered on the farm and transported to market or the kitchen.

Hard-working buttocks baskets are quite similar to twin-bottomed egg baskets, but with even more strongly

M any vintage and antique waste-paper baskets in varied materials are prized by collectors and often considered too beautiful to act as containers for trash—as are many contemporary ones. On a pedestal, a Victorian model holds a vase brimming over with chartreuse lady's mantle. More examples, some featuring lids, are perched atop an old armoire.

WORK BASKETS

More and more homes need a space devoted to paperwork for small business activities, community functions, or general household management. A variety of baskets maintain order—and a casual, homey style—in any work area.

ORGANIZE daily paperwork in flats or trays woven of natural materials. Choose baskets as in and out boxes, or as storage areas for magazines and newspapers with articles to be clipped. Pack a deep basket with shipping and packing materials.

SUBSTITUTE wicker file boxes for small metal file cabinets—their look is softer in the home, and they are lighter weight for moving or stacking as needed.

MIX and match baskets of various sizes and styles for an eclectic, personal environment. Fill them with stationery, paper clips, computer disks, scissors, and rulers.

Wire baskets—some with moveable handles—keep desktop necessities organized. An old gym locker basket holds file folders while a vintage flower frog is now playing the role of a pencil caddy.

pronounced cheeks. One was especially handy when carrying miscellaneous goods to and from market. The handle of the basket was placed over a horse's neck and the depth of each pocket prevented any spillover of the goods.

A wall pocket, with a flat back and rounded front, is designed specifically to hang flush against a flat surface. Heart-shaped ones crafted by Cherokee Indians to store medicinal herbs are now valued for their beauty and featured as ornaments in modern houses.

Elbow baskets, also designed for hanging flat on the wall, take their name from their V-shape that is similar to that of a crooked elbow. Two openings at the top allow for twin displays of dried flowers or dual storage—one side for wooden spoons, perhaps, and the other for whisks, ladles, and spatulas.

Baskets of wire are less traditional, nonwoven and generally manufactured for a specific office or clerical service. Since the beginning of the twentieth century, a vast array of sizes and styles have been made for industry. Thus wire baskets are inexpensive and widely available at tag sales and flea markets. Office supply stores

carry models meant to hold boxes of pens and pencils or supplies of paper. Tiered hanging versions with interconnected baskets store fruits and vegetables so that air can circulate; they are found at kitchen and cookware shops, and hardware stores.

Cat-head baskets of Shaker origin are so called for the four subtle points woven into the shape of the bottom which, when inverted, resembles a cat's head. A very small cat-head is known, naturally, as a kitten-head basket.

Flower-gathering baskets, or trugs, are more or less U-shaped, upturned at the sides, and open at each end to accommodate clippings of ivy or forsythia from the backyard or flower stems of varying lengths as they're snipped from the garden.

Stair-step baskets are woven in the shape of an inverted L and, not surprisingly, fit neatly over two steps. They are useful for collecting items to be transported up or down stairs. Place one on an outdoor staircase and plant it with seasonal shrubs or flowers to welcome guests upon their arrival to the front door.

Adirondack guide packs are durable pot-bellied baskets designed in the Adirondack Mountains in New York State for use by nineteenth-century backpackers. The supply of vintage specimens is dwindling due to their recent

A large wire basket resting on a wheeled stand (above) is filled with a fabric designer's finished pillows, and slips easily between the showroom and studio. A smaller inverted Λ-line model (opposite) holds spools of colored fabrics and trimmings waiting their turn in future projects.

Woven sometime around 1850, an oak splint basket was probably carried by its original owner to market somewhere in Pennsylvania. Now it is a fitting container for a centerpiece of lemons in a country kitchen. The olive-green paint on the basket's base rim, top rim, and handle was likely added twenty or thirty years after the basket was made. The wide handle allowed for a more comfortable grip; the extra base helped extend the container's lifetime.

B askets are the perfect kitchen accessory as they hold an assortment of cooking staples. Red and white potatoes and garlic bulbs are nestled snugly in pull-out baskets which boldly contrast with the pink shelving (opposite). A wide-splint gathering basket conveniently holds oils, vinegars, sauces, and other essential supplies for cooking and grilling (above). The handled basket easily carries all favorite condiments to the backyard grill or picnic table.

popularity as collectibles. Look for baskets woven of strong materials such as ash splints or other hardwoods, with the characteristic bulbous front. Leather or good-quality canvas straps and a fitted lid are also valued assets.

Nantucket lightship baskets are round or oval baskets of rattan or other cane tightly woven over oak or ash, often fitted with a swing (not stationary) handle and a wooden base. Men stationed aboard coastal lightships shaped wood left over from ship repairs into bases and wove the baskets to fill the long idle hours during their watches.

The berry basket is another example that was born of a specific need—in this case, gathering. Strawberries, blackberries, and raspberries collected from the fields, even grapes snipped from the vine, are placed in small handled baskets, then carried home to be baked in pies or served on waffles. The baskets are constructed of wide splints plaited fairly close together to create a weave that is free of gaps through which the fruits could accidentally slip. Berry baskets are occasionally made only of wide-splint spokes for a more rustic look.

Bushel baskets are much larger containers that often have the same composition as weaver-free berry baskets. If weavers are used, they are simple splints or even wires lashed as bands around the outside of the basket.

Utilitarian vessels, most bushel baskets are quickly constructed for carrying fresh corn, ripe tomatoes, apples, and other produce that needs to be transported from field to market without being crushed or damaged.

VERSATILE FLATS

Flat baskets, new and old, come in countless shapes and sizes. A flat basket such as a cradle board once played an integral part in daily life. Placed on the back, a cradle board allowed a Native American woman to tend to traditional chores such as cooking, cleaning, and gathering local fruits and nuts while also protecting her children. In coffee-growing regions such as parts of Central and South America, the flat side of the basket is strapped to one's back, leaving the hands free to gather coffee beans. In other regions, these flat gathering baskets help to sort crops such as tea leaves and to separate grains.

Today, flat baskets have myriad uses at home. Any one can be a tray for serving breakfast in bed or for presenting party food. Specially sized baskets hold casserole dishes to protect a wooden tabletop or other delicate surface.

Arrange several shallow baskets on a coffee table to sort stacks of magazines by title or topic, to hold newspa-

A n assortment of pale wood-splint baskets in a variety of sizes is a fresh and orderly greeting where one might expect to find the usual refrigerator hodge-podge. Though woven of lightweight material, the baskets have reinforced rims and handles that make them sturdy enough to withstand daily contact.

W oven trays with handles make excellent, decidedly casual serving tools for entertaining. The basket's base should be flat and sturdy enough to hold stemware and other fragile pieces securely. If the woven bottom is too nubby, line the tray with a board cut to fit, a baking sheet, or even a mirror. Dress the bottom with a linen tray towel or remnant of handsome fabric. A basket tray will almost always be lighter than a wood or metal tray.

or crossword puzzle books, and to keep needlework projects and their yarns at the ready.

Flat baskets also work well to organize miscellaneous utensils that won't fit neatly into compartmentalized holders. In bedrooms and bathrooms, baskets attractively store cosmetics, perfumes, and small necessities. In the family room, flat baskets organize art supplies, puzzle pieces, and remote control devices.

Flat baskets with especially well-crafted or unique weaves are beautiful even when they are empty—either mounted on the wall or arranged, leaning, on a mantel or picture ledge.

FOR THE BEDROOM

Baskets make warm and natural additions to any bedroom. They offer open yet orderly storage that accommodates seasonal requirements (organizing woolen scarves and gloves), personal interests (protecting photographs and souvenirs destined for a scrapbook), and family changes (providing sleeping quarters for a new puppy). Their myriad sizes and shapes can be adapted to fit and maximize any amount of space. An old picnic hamper, for example, is an attractive catch-all for bedtime reading and

T*he convenience of open shelving is greatly enhanced by baskets that can be pulled out like drawers—and even carried directly to a counter or table. In a corner, new willow storage baskets with sturdy dowels lashed to their grips conceal a supply of linens and extra bedroom staples. The two-handled basket holds a potted boxwood atop a wicker stool, bringing the texture and color of the drawers out to infuse the whole room.*

doubles nicely as a bedside table or a blanket chest at the foot of the bed.

You may want to create a chest of drawers from an arrangement of baskets and shelves. If you have built-in or ready-made shelving, pull-out baskets are the most attractive way to make the most of every inch of these wide, deep storage spaces. To prevent scratching the shelves and wear and tear on the bottom of a basket, tack soft cloth or a length of felt underneath.

In an awkward corner, stack cube-shaped baskets on their sides to form a freestanding tiered tower. Fill one with hardcover books, or boxes of games in a child's bedroom or play room. In a clothes closet, organize shoes, boots, and accessories in separate baskets.

Generously sized baskets offer simultaneous storage and display for quilts, blankets, pillows, and other bulky items. Covered baskets bring a pleasing aesthetic to a bedroom while concealing shoes and caps, knickknacks waiting to find a home, and various pieces of memorabilia. If the basket doesn't have its own cover, a stylist's trick of the trade is to top the stored miscellany with a pretty pillow, an artfully arranged throw, an inverted basket, a framed mirror, or even a wide-brimmed plaited-straw hat.

Ingenious uses for baskets are limitless. To create a

A roomy basket (opposite) turns a cold-weather necessity—extra blankets—into a decorating luxury. The generous basket is in keeping with the scale of a bedroom notable for its wide floorboards and bold throw pillows. A wickerwork basket filled with like-colored cable-knit sweaters complements the decor in an all-white bedroom (above).

small storage table, cover the lid of a woven trunk with a wooden plank or a cut-to-size piece of glass to protect the weave of the basket and provide stability. Position the basket at the side of a slipper chair or chaise and it is an end table; in front of a boudoir loveseat, it is a coffee table. Either way, it affords storage for the bedroom's odds and ends: stationery for correspondence, crafts supplies, cameras and binoculars, and all those manuals and remote controls for the television, video cassette recorder, telephones, and stereo equipment.

Transform hourglass-shaped baskets into pedestals. Cover them with wood or glass and stand a vase filled with flowers or reeds on top. Take advantage of the transparency of the glass by filling the basket with pebbles, marbles, or colorful handblown glass balls. Create a false bottom an inch or two down to hold less filler and allow the basket to remain lightweight.

In a child's bedroom, rely on large baskets as great catch-all alternatives to the standard toy chest. Fill them with stuffed animal collections, wardrobes of dolls' clothes, and toy cars and trucks. Designate one durable basket near the bureau as a shoe catcher to end those frantic before-school searches for footwear—and another lidded basket in a corner for catching dirty clothing.

L ined effortlessly with a pretty hemstitched linen napkin, a small woven willow tray with a braided rim is beautifully suited for a romantic breakfast or a light afternoon snack. Small pots of steaming hot tea, fresh cream, ripe raspberries in meringue, and a handful of pink, yellow, and white roses in a tiny glass vase make the sweetest of gestures when delivered on a cozy winter afternoon.

BUYING BASKETS

If you look around your house you may be surprised to find that you have many more baskets than you realized—and that you already have the beginnings of a pleasing collection. If you're setting out to acquire a basket for everyday use or to start a more ambitious collection, consider a few points before making your selection.

What will the basket's use be? If it's an object of beauty destined only for decoration or display, choose what pleases your eye. A basket for storing or toting, however, must be well-made and sturdy.

How do you tell if the basket is well made? The splices where weavings overlap should be concealed inside. The weave should be smooth, consistent, and free of crooked spots. Patterns should be well-positioned and straight except for intentionally rough-and-rustic or artistic originals, where quirky asymmetry may be the key to the basket's charming character.

How will the basket wear? Handles, rims, and bases should be securely lashed on or woven in, or fastened with good-quality hardware—preferably not stapled or glued.

Are the details appealing? Pay attention to subtleties such as intricate weaves, nicely carved handles, and unusual shapes and materials.

O riginally designed to keep notions, ribbons, and various fabrics accessible beside a chair or a work table, a sewing stand is a charming relic of another time. It now serves as convenient storage for a supply of toilet tissue, hand towels, and glass canisters of washroom necessities. Newly manufactured double-tiered stands similar to this one are widely available.

95

What is its condition? When evaluating an antique basket, examine it from all sides to rule out brittleness, major breaks, stains, or a sagging shape. But some smooth wear on the bottom, a mellow patina, a darkening of the handle where it was held add character to a vintage basket.

Who made it and when? As with any antique, baskets that can be authenticated as the work of a respected craftsperson or as an original of a certain era will likely have more intrinsic value. Look for stamps or brands on the bottom of old baskets. Since basketry has gained respect as an artform, the most sought-after basket makers proudly sign their work. Bear in mind that every basket—whether a signed original or a plain container for a fruit arrangement—was handmade by somebody.

C olors accent the naturally woody palette of baskets for a surefire decorating technique. A diagonally plaited splintwork basket is painted with a subtle blue wash to coordinate with an antique desk at the bottom of a sunny stairway. A basket at the head and foot of each stairway will prove endlessly helpful, holding items meant to move from one floor to another until a family member is next passing by.

MAKING REPAIRS

Signs of wear and tear may be charming in an antique basket, but you might consider undertaking minor repairs to prevent further damage, especially if the basket serves a practical as well as a decorative purpose. First, evaluate if you'll be able to mend the area inconspicuously. If not, it might be preferable to simply display the basket, flaws and all, or at least to situate the basket so its best side faces out.

COMING AND GOING

POSITION baskets to expand storage and keep daily life running smoothly, in each entry area and in mud rooms. Covered porches receive more than their fair share of the essentials that flow in and out of a house.

CATEGORIZE outdoor gear in oversized heavy-duty baskets—in-line skates and helmets in one; tennis rackets and assorted balls in a second; rain boots and umbrellas in a third—or assign one basket for each family member.

USE flat or trug baskets on an entry table to collect incoming or outgoing mail, car and house keys, the dog's leash, homework assignments and school books, or whatever comes in and must later go out again.

TURN the top shelf in a hall closet into organized hat, scarf, glove, and mitten drawers with baskets that extend to the back of the shelf. Wire baskets are particularly suited to this task, as their contents are easily visible.

On newer baskets, minor repairs can usually be accomplished by a fairly knowledgeable weaver. Matching the materials accurately is the key to completing successful repairs. Fortunately, there are more basket material supply sources than ever before. Many museums can locate a source for you, and better crafts shows or guilds also can lead you in the right direction.

Ideally, the repair of an antique basket should be handled by a professional. Sometimes, in fact, the best approach is to leave a valuable basket in its found condition. In many cases, repairing or replacing any of the material would diminish the basket's value, just as repair-

N ow enjoying a second career holding bike helmets and other sports gear, the openwork willow baskets under an extra-long entry hall table started life offering baguettes and other long loaves in French bakeries. A market basket, once used by European women to carry fresh breads and produce home daily, hangs ready on the doorknob to collect videos and library books to be returned.

A woven grass bag popular in Florence, Italy, typifies the soft-sided market basket Europeans favor (opposite). A Mexican flower mat is designed for rolling around freshly cut blossoms at the flower market to carry home. A roll-up mat also serves as easy-tote beach seating or as a textured tablecloth. Oval chicken-wire baskets stored alongside the potting shed (above) are sturdy outdoor holders for extra terra-cotta dry wells.

ing or refinishing certain pieces of antique furniture may severely compromise their value.

If you decide to try some repairs yourself, start with the most basic fixes. Weavers that have come loose can sometimes be poked back inside the basket with the tip of an awl or a screwdriver. To repair lashing that has unraveled from around a handle or rim, thoroughly dampen the material with a sponge soaked in warm water—this will make the lashing pliable enough to wrap without snapping or cracking. When you've finished rewrapping the material, secure the end by tucking it under the wrapped layers. For wicker furniture, secure a loose end of materials with a small tack, if necessary, but avoid using glue, especially hot-melt glue, which can complicate future repairs because it is extremely difficult to remove.

If the basket has deteriorated to the point where a repair requires additional materials, look for matching reed at a crafts store. Try to weave the new reed in a satisfactory repair. An old basket, however, will probably not take well to new crafts store reed, as it will lack the patina that comes through age and use. One effective option is to look for salvage materials from old baskets that are beyond

feasible repair. Many professional basket repair shops inventory these baskets and may be willing to sell you one if you would like to do the repair yourself. Some ardent collectors keep an eye out for badly damaged baskets. They will purchase these specifically for materials and spare parts for the best of the pieces in their collections.

CARE AND CLEANING

Even if a basket appears to be quite sturdy, an ounce of prevention will generally avert untimely and irreparable damage. As necessary, dust baskets gently with a small, fine-textured brush to keep them clean and free of build-up that will dull the surface of the weave over time. Rinse baskets that are without paint or varnish under a light spray of water. Dry them slowly and carefully; in temperate weather, dry baskets in gentle sunlight to tighten their weave. Moisturize stiff or brittle baskets by letting them spend some time in a humid room, such as a bathroom with the shower running or a covered outdoor porch during a mild rainstorm.

Rotate baskets that are left hanging to prevent continuous stress and wear on the same portion of the handles. Always protect baskets made of natural materials by keep-

A vintage wicker bicycle basket (opposite) that attaches to the handlebars has never really diminished in practicality or beauty. In days past, farm wives carried dessert to the neighborhood barn raising or church social in a pie basket (above). Vintage single pie carriers can be found in antiques shops; an antique double, or two-story, version is a rare find.

In the 1890s, professional Adirondack Mountain guides carried a canoeing tea service (opposite) when hosting wealthy clients; picnicking with one today is equally as extravagant. The widely spaced spokes of a deep open-work iron basket (above) make it rather impractical for gathering nuts and berries; however, it is perfect for collecting and storing apples.

ing them out of direct sunlight and its deteriorating effects. Also avoid extreme temperature fluctuations, hot or cold, as they will stress a basket's delicate composition.

NEW AND "VINTAGE" FINISHES

If you want to give a basket a new finish, there are a few hard and fast rules. Of course, different materials will respond in individual ways to stains, dyes, and paints. Wood fibers, for example, respond well to most finishes. Oil-based stains are effective, but experiment with other substances, too, such as vegetable dyes. Many new products—both the baskets and the dyes and stains—are quite affordable. Intricately woven wicker is easily and evenly colored with high-grade spray-paint; apply two or three light coats to avoid drips. Even fabric dyes will work on some baskets. Containers made from grasses are usually left to age naturally; however, Native Americans of the Southwest are quite adept at dying beargrass.

If you weave baskets yourself, you have even more choices. Pine needles, for instance, dye beautifully. But like all fine materials, they should be dyed before weaving, for they are usually coiled, and you may want bindings to remain natural or dyed another color.

Wood-splint baskets, after being freshly woven, look far more finished if the loose fibers are removed. This can be accomplished in numerous ways, with small scissors or clippers, or even dampening the basket and very carefully burning the edges of the wayward fibers.

If you cannot afford a collection of genuine antique baskets, do not hesitate to achieve the rustic look you desire with baskets you already have or can pick up for a song at import shops, tag sales, and flea markets. A primary characteristic of a vintage basket is its mellow patina, or deepening of color, that occurs as it ages. Approximate this effect by applying dye to darken a natural basket.

If you want to achieve the appearance of an antique painted basket, choose flat paint, which predated shiny enamels. A modern version of milk paint, which dates from Colonial times, is available in paint shops, and gives an authentic finish. Gold or bronze paint, sparingly applied, also creates the look of a patina. For a timeworn effect, dip a cotton rag into the paint, and wipe the color sparingly on the basket, undercoating the handle, where paint would have naturally worn away. With a clean cloth, remove any excess paint in the corners or between weaves. Finish the basket with a light rubbing with fine sandpaper to simulate the appearance of desirable age and wear.

A seamstress' workstation is a fitting place for a collection of baskets. Knitting needles, skeins of yarn, and spools of thread are stored in baskets of various sizes, shapes, and even colors. When you are buying baskets for a hobby like sewing, select a variety of sizes; the size will dictate what you should store inside it—shiny plastic buttons for dolls' eyes in a tiny basket, antique buttons in a small one, and fabric swatches in one that is larger still.

glossary

BASE: a flat and sturdy piece of woven or coiled material that forms the bottom of the basket. The base may also be a separate piece of wood with holes into which the spokes are inserted.

CANE: the outer bark of rattan or another type of reed. Split away from the core and smoothed into strips, it is employed for furniture caning or basket weaving.

COILING: a form of basketry in which flexible yet sturdy material is looped into an ever-enlarging spiral. It is bound together by stitching, and each twist is lashed to the one before.

FEET: external attachments or shapes that are woven into the underside of the basket to lift it off the ground for better air circulation, to enhance stability or durability, or just to add a decorative finish. The feet are often called *skeds*.

FOUNDATION: material that is bundled, wound, and then stitched together to form long spirals that create a coilwork basket.

HANDLES: an optional part of the basket to facilitate grasping, lifting, and carrying. Some are simply holes intentionally woven into the sides of the basket; some are actual woven loops. Swing handles are made of a woven or wooden material and then hinged to fold flat to the basket.

MOLD: a solid form, often constructed of wood, around which a basket is woven to maintain a consistent shape among pieces. Puzzle molds consist of numerous pieces for removal once a desired shape is achieved.

PLAITING: a type of weave in which flat, ribbon-like, same-sized pieces of a material are criss-crossed in an even over-and-under pattern of intersections. Plaiting can also be woven in a diagonal pattern.

RATTAN: a Southeast-Asian tropical palm vine that resembles bamboo and bears a solid core and flexible bark.

REED: the rattan core that is split into numerous cuts of flat or round pieces used mainly for basket weaving. Any type of slender tall grass with lengthy jointed stems, similarly cut, is considered to be reed.

RIM: the upper edge of the basket that gives stability and a finished edge. The rim is formed by trimming and folding over the weavers when the basket reaches its desired height, by weaving around a separate piece of wood or material, or by adding a separate woven piece–a braided edge, for instance.

SPLINTS: flat thin strips of hardwoods such as ash, oak, and poplar that are used as weavers and sometimes as spokes. Splints are sliced from tree trunks and soaked in water until they are sufficiently flexible for weaving. When they are very finely split, wood splints are used as highly decorative curls for the design of the exterior.

SPOKES: the longitudinal ribs that form the upright skeleton of the basket in the process of twining. Spokes are commonly referred to as the *warp* of a basket.

TWINING: basket making in which two or more strands of weavers are passed continually over and under the spokes.

WEAVERS: the lateral crosspieces that move around the spokes, to form the fabric, or weave, of the basket in twining. Weavers are also called *weft*.

WICKERWORK: a manner of weaving in which one weaver is passed continually over and under the spokes. The material in wickerwork is often rounded.

index